THOMAS WOODSMAN

HEAD SHOTS

WORK IN ANY

CALIBER

I am admittedly somewhat pensive about presenting the information I have gathered for this book. But, with all of the discontent, terroristic activity and social upheaval all around the world today I decided that it would be a good topic to address so I have put into book form my research and thoughts in order to present to you, my readers, what I believe to be vitally important information that could perhaps someday save your life.

I am not a radical by any stretch of the imagination. I do however enjoy going to the local shooting range at times to stay current on my shooting skills but my intent is not, nor has it ever been, to harm anyone out of malice. Rather, I practice to hone my skills so that in the event I would have to defend myself, my family or others around me I will be able to do so with the confidence needed to act swiftly, effectively and as best I can without harming any innocent bystanders.

Having said that, I will now present to you information that is readily available to the general public but rarely put into book form in an orderly fashion. My intent is to educate. Nothing more, nothing less.

Rather than beginning this book by talking about shooting skills I think it is important to talk first about why it is that you have gotten yourself into a situation that could turn into something that could be "bad for your health."

What Is Situational Awareness and Why Is It So Important?

You either could have or should have had enough common sense to stay out of the area you're in, the situation you've stumbled into or the unfortunate circumstance that has taken you totally by surprise.

I never ever go into a public place and sit with my back to the door. Also, I always scan the area and determine where the quickest exit might be should I need to use it. I am constantly aware of people around me and note their dress, their tone of voice while speaking to others well as their 'mood' or demeanor etc. If I am the least bit uncomfortable with what I'm seeing or hearing my next move is to leave. No body needs the hassle of what could (but likely won't) happen but regardless I am not willing to put anyone with me in a situation that could cause them any type of harm.

Certainly this might sound a little on the paranoid side but it is also putting me on the safe side of life as opposed to simply ignoring warning signals and taking a chance that something or someone could present danger. I simply am not willing to take the chance. Are you?

My career spanned over twenty years as a probation/parole agent for a large state agency. Through the years I had to go through extensive training as it related to situational awareness, self defense techniques as well as armed self defense with a variety of weapons and tools. Most people aren't afforded this training. Even more than that though I felt fortunate that I never once had to draw a weapon and use it to defend myself or my partners in any type of active shooter situation. Indeed there were times when weapons were drawn as sometimes you must be a little bit ahead of the curve as it relates to your safety. Clearing areas, addressing issues that suddenly come up etc. is no easy task. Situational awareness was not only a nice thing to have it was a must.

You should also be aware of what is going on around you. Sometimes that is all it takes to keep yourself safe. If it feels bad it likely is bad and the best and smartest thing you can do is leave immediately. Problem solved.

Lets go a little deeper now into the topic of situational awareness and learn some skills that could save your life.

To learn how to maintain situation awareness I have spoken in depth with many experts in the field and recorded then transcribed our interviews. From this point forward in our discussion about situational awareness I'm going to present what they, as experts in the field, had to say. I think you'll find what they have to say both entertaining as well as educational.

INTERVIEW #1:

Situational Awareness - The Most Important Thing

The one thing that will absolutely guarantee you come out on the losing end of a confrontation is not being aware of your surrounds and failing to position yourself accordingly.

You must remain aware and provide yourself with the best positioning the environment has to offer. Most of the time physical altercations build up over a period of time. That is because people who become aggressive have to talk themselves into action. They do this primarily by trying to elicit a gesture or insult from you that will make them mad enough to get past that fear in the pit of their stomach. Knowing this, even if an altercation is unavoidable, means you can buy enough time to take the fight to a place where you have an inherent advantage.

The first thing you need to assess is how many possible assailants will be involved. Key in on body language. A tense stance, unwavering attention to you and the primary assailants back and forth, or a strong family resemblance are all things to look for. Two on one fights are never fun, and more than that just plain hurts no matter who wins.

In the case that there is more than one person you feel may jump in, you need to take the time during the buildup to position all assailants in front of you. Giving one your back will only give that person enough courage to blindside you. To do this technique properly without giving away your intent, you have to appear more interested in something besides your primary assailant. This lets you move about without drawing too much attention to what you're doing. It also gives the assailant a chance to lose interest.

Pick your spot wisely. If you can funnel multiple attackers in a tight location, you're back to one on one odds since two people won't have room to attack at the same time. Also if you can incapacitate an assailant with a joint lock, you can use their body as a shield. If at this point you still cannot remove yourself safely from the situation, quickly torque whatever joint you have hold of, remove that person from the fight, and move on to the next closest attacker.

The earlier you recognize a dangerous situation, the better your chances of walking away from it. Practice your situational awareness when you're out in public. Break the habit of tunnel visioning and tuning people out. Do this with your family and teach your kids. Ask them what color shirt the person that just walked past had on. When everyone gets good at that, step it up to hair color. When everyone gets to the point where they can tell you what eye color the person had, you and your family will be in the 1% of the population that actually pays attention to their surroundings and one step closer to never becoming a victim.

INTERVIEW #2:

Sometimes I stand amazed. Amazed at how a simple state of mind can somehow elude most people. Not all people, but it seems most. I am talking about situational awareness; what is going on around you. There are so many people working, walking, and functioning in potentially busy or dangerous areas that have no idea what is going on around them. I don't really remember anyone teaching me this concept, nor was I formally trained for it either. I guess soldiers in the military have understood it best, either pay attention to what's around you, or what's around you will kill you. Maybe that's why drill instructors scream so much, they are trying to get you to pay attention. But most of us are not facing the threat of death so its somewhat eluding.

If you work in a commercial workshop, the dangers of the job can be evident. Paying attention to a machine that has blades that are capable of removing parts of your body with amazing speed sobers you somewhat to the thought of safety and awareness. Driving a car can be just as good an example. How many times have you drifted off into deep thought to suddenly realize you are at your exit? People that multi task behind the wheel have no idea what is going on in the lane next to them. Some of the best drivers I know, don't really pay attention to the car at the intersection, they are looking at the driver to see if they are paying attention.

We can be so out to lunch. I notice this even more so in the public setting. It's not just the workplace that we can be unaware of our surroundings. Try walking through a public airport. It is amazing at the amount of people that cannot even comprehend the fact that there are other people walking in the same space, in the same lines, or trying to get from point A to B. Yet they wander through the terminal in a meandering state of mind, alone in the universe so to speak. . If you're going to walk, walk with purpose. I know who is next to me, and I am capable of blending into a rhythm of movement that is both efficient and harmonious. It's awareness, nothing more, nothing less. I hate it when someone labels me hyper or "type A" simply because I am diligent. In fact if you look around, alert mindful people are the ones that get promoted in the job place. Sure other factors weigh in, but most of the world cannot even show up on time.

It would seem that wild animals have a good grasp of this concept. Mother Nature surely trained them well in order to survive. But somehow we evolved our way out of it. So how is your situational awareness? Does any of this sound familiar? Have you ever even heard of this concept? . If you're mindful and alert you know what I am talking about. My mother said it's being considerate, maybe that's what it boils down too. I call it self preservation.

INTERVIEW #3:

Developing Astute Awareness

Awareness is the knowledge or perception of a situation or fact; to be concerned and well informed about a particular situation or development.

Astute is defined as having or showing an ability to accurately assess situations or people and turn this to one's advantage.

If you have ever read practically ANY self-defense literature or taken a class for personal safety and protection, rest assured you have heard the terms "awareness" or "situational awareness" countless times. Most experts agree that awareness is one of the most important and preventative aspects of self-defense methodology, but I feel there is more to the overall concept that most instructors and courses fail to address. Situational awareness and general awareness of your environment is unquestionably important, but a thorough knowledge of criminal psychology and a solid understanding of how, why, where, and when criminals attack, holds critical significance. Let's do a quick exercise to illustrate what I'm referring to, and please take a personal inventory of your answers to the following questions:

What are the strongest body language indicators of a violent attacker?

Where, when and how are sexual assaults most likely to occur?

What are the top 3 reported characteristics criminals look for in a victim?

Do verbal deescalation techniques work against serial rapists or stalkers?

The answers to these questions are specifically linked to criminal psychology and hopefully it becomes increasingly evident that any instructor who merely teaches you to "be aware of your surroundings" is providing insufficient ideology and inferior training. When you can decipher and predict criminal psychological behaviors such as, how a murderer selects a his victims, or why a thief targets a particular housing complex, or where an attacker prefers to conceal weapons on his body, you will drastically enhance your astute awareness and decrease the likelihood of experiencing or succumbing to a violent attack.

To further clarify why I prefer the term astute awareness rather than situational awareness, it is largely due to the actual definition and meaning of the words. If you look back to my opening statement today you will see that astute is defined as having or showing an ability to accurately assess situations or people and turn this to one's advantage. In terms of self-defense and personal protection ideology, the language in that definition is remarkably relevant and suitable. Specifically the part about accurately assessing situations or people, and to a greater extent, turning the assessment into an advantage. This is an important point to digest and one that should not be forgotten. After all, an advantage is a condition or circumstance that puts one in a favorable or superior position. It is critical for the defense-minded individual to not only be aware of situational circumstances and their environment, but also to understand the psychology of human behavior (especially the deviant, deranged and psychotic members of society) and assimilate that information in way that creates a safer more secure world for you and your loved ones. On the most basic level, we will use our astute awareness to create a preventative and reactionary advantage over potentially dangerous individuals.

In my humble opinion, the entire purpose behind awareness training is essentially to provide an individual with an opportunity to secure an advantage over a potential adversary or threat. What this really boils down to is threat recognition and reaction time. There is an incredibly important and reputable training exercise, known as the Tueller Drill or Tueller Principle, that has established respect and notoriety within the law enforcement, military, and armed civilian communities. For those unfamiliar with the exercise, it was a drill created by former police Lieutenant and renowned firearms instructor Dennis Tueller. While conducting police recruit draw-and-fire training drills from a distance of seven yards, an important question was asked by one of the academy recruits- how close is an armed attacker (e.g. knife, club, crowbar, machete) allowed to approach before the use of deadly force is justified to stop the assault?

From previous distance-time shooting evaluations, it was established that the average time required to draw a pistol, acquire an object, fire the weapon and hit the target at seven yards, was approximately 1.5 seconds from an external belt holster. To adequately address the use-of-deadly-force question posed by the new police recruit, an experiment was set up to calculate how much time it took a potential armed attacker to cover the same distance, seven yards. The analysis consisted of one officer playing the role of the "bad guy" and another recruit playing the role of the "startled officer"; they were positioned 21 feet apart (seven yards), and the timer started from the very instant the role-player bad guy initiated movement and the timer stopped when contact was made with the startled officer. As Sgt. Tueller revealed, "I was quite stunned to discover that the time was roughly 1.5 seconds!" The same stopwatch exercise was executed with all recruits from that class (e.g. younger, older, larger, smaller, male and female) and all of them could sprint that seven yards distance at an average of 1.5 seconds. Sgt. Tueller's conclusion is enlightening,

"What we found was that if you're ready and if everything goes perfectly, you might get the gun out and get a shot off before the bad guy role-player makes contact. That is not good enough! Shooting does not stop the action."

So what exactly does the Tueller Drill have to do with awareness training and helping you survive a violent street attack?

First, seven yards is significant distance and in a large portion of documented and realistic physical or sexual assaults, you won't be afforded the luxury of a 21-foot warning or alert. According to a reputable and thorough analysis performed by Tom Givens (Owner & Instructor at Rangemaster), it was found that data collected from 58 actual civilian self-defense shooting incidents reveals that 89.6% of the conflicts occurred at a distance of LESS THAN 5 YARDS! In fact, 86.2% took place in the 3-5 yards range {9 to 15 feet}. By objectively examining these numbers and envisioning a 9-15 foot circle of safety around your body, hopefully you will understand and accept the fact that on a daily basis someone could be close enough to violently attack you, without you ever being aware of their presence. For example:

Entering and standing in an elevator at work, a hotel, a government building, or an apartment complex.

Waiting in line at a restaurant, movie theater, sporting event, grocery store, gas station, or a bank.

Attending a parade, walking through the local farmer's market, visiting historical landmarks.

Second, as Sgt. Tueller astutely pointed out, shooting does not stop the forward progression, action and lethal ability of a charging attacker.

For instance, envision a dangerous and violent assailant wielding a razor-sharp knife, that threat is still capable of inflicting potentially lethal stab wounds if your defensive measures do not incapacitate them immediately.

There are several enlightening articles and published studies that document the surprising survivability of gunshot victims {e.g. Kenny Vaughn, shot 20 times; Joseph Guzman, shot 19 times}. In a study entitled Penetrating Cardiac Injuries, conducted by the Harborview Injury Prevention Center, of 41 cardiac gunshot wound victims that remained alive long enough to be transported to a trauma center, 29.3% of them survived.

A key point to consider is that 41 people who received gunshot wounds to the HEART, still had the ability and time to continue a potential attack and survived long enough to be transported to a hospital.

Third, how you choose to carry your defensive weapon (e.g. inside the waistband, outside waistband, ankle holster, shoulder holster, purse or bag), will significantly affect your weapon deployment and utilization time. The recruits in the Tueller study were specifically trained how to use their sidearm, they were drawing from an exterior and easily accessible belt holster, and their average time was 1.5 seconds. If you don't extensively practice drawing from concealment, incorporate dry-fire drills with trigger reset, include moving while drawing or reloading, and integrate simulated stress scenarios, that 1.5 seconds will most certainly be exaggerated.

Regardless of whether or not you agree or disagree with the findings and principles derived from the Tueller drill, there is one indisputable truth- the sooner you recognize a threat, the more distance and reaction time you will have to react; the more reaction time you can procure, the better chance you will have to defend and survive an attack.

Alright. There is much more that could be said about situational and astute awareness methods and techniques but my intent is not to give you a totally in depth training as much as it is to make you more aware of what is required of you as it relates to personal safety and how to better achieve it.

I am going to continue with the interview transcripts in the next section as I firmly believe that getting more than a one-sided opinion is very important.

Lets move on now to another subject; Home Defense.

Some of what I am going to provide within the next few pages will perhaps make you uncomfortable. After all, you have second amendments rights, the Castle law backs you up as you defend your home and many other alleged rights to stand your ground come to mind. But, keep reading and you'll find some interesting thoughts, situations etc. that might help you make better and wiser choices as you determine how to defend your home in a self defense situation. If you decide you don't agree with what I am saying that is okay. I had to go through many hours of deep self examination as I tried to come up with a viable and effective self defense plan. You should too and then do what is best for you.

INTERVIEW #4:

Home Defense - What Are Your Options?

Over the years I have heard many people ask, "What is the best way for me to protect my home?" The responses always intrigued me. Depending upon who you ask, you will get many different answers. A Gun Store Owner will tell you that a firearm is the way to go, but I need to tell you that for the majority of families a firearm can actually place you in more harm than if you were unarmed.

There are many factors that I use to back up this statement. First, there are the legal issues associated with obtaining a license to possess a firearm. Second, a firearm is a deadly weapon. Are you prepared to pick up that gun, take aim at a home intruder and pull the trigger? You'd better be sure because if you hesitate it is likely that the tables will be turned and that gun will be used against you and your family. Third, what if you accidentally discharge that firearm either in a perceived defensive encounter, or while cleaning or practicing? The resulting mess will result in tragedy, grief, and more than likely arrest, criminal charges, and possibly even incarceration. So if after deciding you are ready to own a firearm for home defense and I truly support your right to make that decision, please take the necessary steps to educate yourself, train yourself both in tactics as well as in mental preparedness, and most important of all make sure you are completely familiar with the use and care of your firearm. If you have young children at home there is also the matter of securing your handgun when not in use.

So where does all this leave you? In my opinion you have several very good options and they fall directly into the Non-Lethal Personal Defense category and are comprised of Electronic Control Devices more commonly know as Stun Guns or Tasers and Personal Defense Sprays such as Pepper Spray.

Choosing any of these less than lethal options affords you very good protection for yourself, your family and your property. With a defense spray or Stun Gun, your attacker is rendered virtually helpless, providing you with valuable time to get to safety and notify the authorities. In the event of an accidental discharge or a mis-identified threat, well all you are faced with is a bit of embarrassment and the recipient, well a bit of discomfort. All of this pales in comparison to shooting someone accidentally with a firearm.

In the end the choice is yours. I have seen numerous tragedies relating to the misuse of a firearm. Lives lost, families broken apart and even criminal charges of negligence. I support the right to keep and bear arms; I just think that too many people don't fully understand the responsibility that comes with it.

INTERVIEW #5:

Home Defense During Riots, Looting and Civil Unrest

Most people think they will always be safe and never have to worry about riots, looting or civil unrest. However, most people also figured that the US would always be solvent, as opposed to becoming the biggest debtor nation in the history of the world. With the greatest number of people ever now receiving government assistance, what will happen when the government can no longer cut those checks.

Equally as bad, what will happen when the checks people receive lose their purchasing power due to hyperinflation? We are living in times unlike any other in history, where generations of Americans have grown up totally financially dependent upon the government, and the government is broke. History has taught us that when people lose hope, they take to the streets, and desperate people do desperate things.

Now Is The Time To Plan Home Defense

It takes very little planning now to enact some steps that can literally save your life if/when riots and looting strike your area. Contrary to popular opinion, you don't necessarily needs guns to protect yourself, your home and your loved ones from rioters or looters. Not if you are smart. The key is to "harden your house" to make is a less attractive target and also a more difficult place to loot. You won't have to brandish a firearm if looters never choose your house. The time to take these steps is now, when there is no emergency.

The first thing to do is to employ passive measures to make your house less of a target. Just as the overwhelming majority of home invasions happen through the front door, your front door communicates a lot to would-be looters. If your outer door is the kind with decorative steel instead of a large pane of glass, it looks much less inviting. So your first step of "house hardening" should be to look at replacing your front door. In addition, the installation of "The Door Club" is a $40 investment that will make your door nearly impossible to kick in, and it will take less than an hour to install. This way, when you are home and the door club is in place, anyone wanting to come in your front door will be stopped, or at the very least delayed greatly, even if they have a battering ram that the police use.

Safety Is Beautiful

Once your front door is secured, both by looking secure with a steel outer door, and by being very secure with a Door Club, turn your attention to your front windows. It is NOT necessary to install burglar bars, which most people find less than attractive. A great way to keep people from coming in your windows is by planting rose bushes! Anyone who has picked roses knows from painful experience that a bush full of sharp thorns is NOT an obstacle that you will take lightly. Planting rose bushes is a very modest investment - they can be purchased for under ten dollars each and they grow and grow. Anyone starting to go through your roses to get to your window will soon stop.

A More Fiendish Deterrent

While you are waiting for your roses to grow, or if there is an emergency before you have time to plant them, boards like 2 x 4's with nails sticking up will do the same thing. They can be either fastened to the window sill to let those approaching know what they are in for, or they can be placed on the ground under the windows with a half-inch of dirt concealing them, so that looters will discover them the hard way.

Your Final Line of Defense

If you have followed the steps above, your home is hardened and is much less likely to be burglarized or looted. However, there is always the chance that an unwelcome guest could get inside and threaten the safety of you and your family. If you don't have a firearm and some training, there is a simple non-lethal way to protect yourself. Mace or pepper spray is a great way to persuade someone to leave you alone. If you are going to be using it indoors, consider a gel type instead of a spray type, so that the entire room is not fogged with the noxious spray.

Another option is a $4 can of wasp spray. Wasp spray will shoot a stream 20 feet or more, which is a better distance to engage any enemy than up close. If you had several cans, it could possibly be employed from an upstairs window against a small group of troublemakers outside your house. As with lethal force, you must think long and hard about under what circumstances you would employ these weapons, as well as considering any legal ramifications. Attacking someone, even in self-defense, is a serious matter.

INTERVIEW #6:

What Should I Use For Home Defense?

There are those who believe that the largest gun you can get is still too small for home defense. Your options are many. While they can be confusing, they can also point to a unique solution for you. I teach my students that a plan for a home invasion is more important than a specific firearm. A well thought out and rehearsed plan is VERY important.

My dad had a double barreled shotgun and a flash light. We all knew where it was and how to use it. We also knew the predetermined code word we could use to stop any engagement.

A hunting rifle with a really good scope means little in the entry hall of your home. It is a good gun, but is not suited for the task. A shotgun or a very good hand gun makes more sense in this instance.

Most home confrontations happen in less than twenty feet. They are over very quickly and are very loud and violent.

You need to go to the range and practice quick reaction shooting. You can simulate being in your safe room. This, along with rehearsal of your action plan, will save not only time, but your life.

What caliber of gun can you reliably control and quickly get into the fight? Where is it kept? Can you get to it in the dark when you are scared? Do you have ammo loaded in magazines? Where is your safe room?

The answer to these questions may change over time, but the firearm you have in your hand is better than the one you will purchase next month.

There are so many variables to consider and adjust. You may not want a hand cannon. A shotgun or carbine may be a better choice.

A gun is the defense of last resort. Many other items can aid in your defense. Good locks, good lighting, an alarm system, a big dog, or a loud dog, are all items to consider to make your home less inviting. You are in charge of your own security and safety. Think about how you will defend your home from intruders. Defend yourself and your family, not your belongings.

INTERVIEW #7:

The Best Gun (For Home Defense)

As a young hunter then a soldier and former Policeman I've been around weapons most all my life and to me they are just tools machines if you will, machines that have to be respected. But for my wife well... she was just plain scared to the bone of the tools of my trade. But years back hearing me talk with the guys about work and the break-ins, the home invasions and other heinous acts that happen to good people she finally asked me to recommend something she could use.

I instantly replied a Shotgun is your best defense and my little wife launched into a ten minute dissertation as to why that was not her weapon of choice. Once she ended her little tirade I asked her if I could just state my case. I knew I didn't have much time so I said; "Honey" that always helps. I explained the Shotgun I am talking about is small only 26 inches long and it doesn't weigh much and the stellar point about this machine is you don't need bullets. She worries because of the children in the house and those who visit.

I continued a Shotgun is a versatile little gun and has been around in one form or another since guns were invented and since we still use them today it speaks volumes for their consistency.
They can fire dangerous loads sure, but they can also shoot out bean bags or simply blanks. The point I was trying to make was nearly all men especially the bad guys know what a Shotgun is and the sight of the weapon can make a big mean nasty man turn to mush and when you charge the gun or put a bullet in the chamber to shoot it. The Shotgun has a distinct sound kind of a loud click slam whack sound. When you hear it you know it and the sound will fill a man with fear.

The next week I took her to the range with her small new pistol grip shotgun and we learned all about the machine I told her if you hear someone breaking in the house or a stranger comes to the door call 911 first then just go back to the bedroom and grab the tool off the hooks above the sliding doors in the closet put two blank rounds in the tube and simply ask the person trying to gain access to the house; Who is It? If the reply is not what you wanted to hear simply say I have a gun and I know how to use it. If they keep trying to come in rack the shotgun CLICK-SLAM at this point be prepared to fire the weapon aim it towards the ceiling and BAM they are very loud let one go. The blanks will do some damage to the ceiling but I can always fix that.

When the Police arrive put the weapon down before answering the door. Today she is comfortable keeping the shotgun loaded with bird shot high up in the closet on hooks the kids don't even know it's up there. For added security she had me install a simple gun lock that can be easily removed. She feels safe and frankly so do I, she evens looks forward to going to the range with me. Wonder if I can talk her into shooting my magnum... Naw!

INTERVIEW #8:

Home Invasion - How Will You Prepare?

The idea of a home invasion is quite terrifying. Just search through news headlines and the stories of these horrific events will make your blood run cold. It is happening closer to home than you would think. The criminals who commit these terrible crimes do not just have robbery on their minds. They usually invade homes in hopes of committing assault, rape, torture, and even murder.

If a violent group of thugs broke into your home and attacked your family would you be able to protect them?

Have you ever asked yourself that *q*uestion? If you have not, then there is no better time than now! Your family and loved ones count on you to protect them. Being able to fulfill this job means being prepared.

Now you may be asking the question, "But how do I get prepared for such an unannounced and unexpected event? I already own a gun and a big dog. Isn't that enough?"

Sadly the answer here is an emphatic NO! The criminals who commit these atrocities are well prepared and you can be sure that they are more than capable of overcoming these two obstacles.

With home invasion statistics on the rise it is absolutely ESSENTIAL to have at the very least basic knowledge and skills in home defense tactics. The good news here is that there is a proven and successful source for this kind of knowledge and training!

A home invasion is not your ordinary crime. Though the criminals may have the art of surprise at the beginning you can hopefully swing that around. Hopefully if you make the right preparations you can flipped the table so that the ball is now in your court!

Think about it:

The intruders do not know the layout of your house as well as you do.

Because of this they do not know what hidden dangers may be lurking around the corner. But as I mentioned before, odds are that these criminals are not going to be stupid. They will have spent much time and preparation, but what you can do is be even more prepared than they are! They will not expect to be facing a combat ready homeowner. The art of surprise could be in your hands.

In these types of situations you can't always count on the police to come to the rescue. You can't always expect the neighbors to hear your screams for help. The most important person to be able to count on is YOURSELF!

INTERVIEW #9:

What You Should Know About Self-Defense and Disasters

A crisis will bring out the best and the worst in people, and you will encounter both good people and bad during a disaster. When the lights go out and people are scrambling to survive there are those ready to take advantage of the situation. Looting begins almost immediately during any crisis. Criminals use the lack of nighttime lighting to their advantage. You have a family and possessions that must be kept safe. Your emergency stockpile is the only thing in some cases keeping you alive and it must be protected. People react to a crisis differently and otherwise law-abiding citizens once they feel desperate may turn to violence to get what they need. You should consider having a firearm or other means of protection during a doomsday situation. If you decide to get a firearm you must take the steps to legally obtain one.

However, simply having a firearm or weapon in the home is not enough. You must know how to handle a weapon, and with the proper training, you will know when to use a weapon. First, if you decide on having a firearm, and you do not need to limit yourself to just one weapon. Consider having multiple means of self-defense weapons from mace to noise makers to firearms. Once you find yourself confronted with an intruder or someone with the intention of doing you bodily harm your objective is to neutralize the threat quickly.

If you choose to have a firearm, a 12-gauge shotgun with an 18.5-inch barrel is an ideal weapon for home defense. The loads can be birdshot or buckshot. You must consider collateral damage so choosing your loads is critical because while you do want penetration you do not want a through and through that can injure someone else in the home or neighborhood. Once you have purchased a weapon you must practice with it at a certified firing range. You must learn to load fire and repeat. Depending on the load and choke settings, shotguns typically are point and shoot. While this may be simplistic it is generally how non-professional will react, they will point and shoot.

People once they realize you have emergency supplies may very well attempt to take them from you and if you do not have a deterrent such as a handgun or shotgun, you and your family will suffer the loss. You cannot have your supplies taken from you during a disaster because it can mean the difference between surviving and not. Additionally, there will be those that simply want to victimize others. Assaults against persons increase during a disaster because tempers flare and people are desperate and others simply take advantage of the chaos.

Make sure you have all of the proper paperwork in order and know what your state laws are on having a weapon on your person and/or in your home. Everyone has the right to defend themselves, their families and their property. Whether or not you decide that owning a firearm is the best method for your home defense is a difficult decision that must be made through careful consideration. Even if you decide against owning a firearm, you should have another means of defense.

INTERVIEW #10:

Self Defense in a Deteriorating Economy

Many people think that social collapse looks something like a scene from the old Road Warrior movie starring Mel Gibson where bands of lawless psychopaths rule their claimed territory like warlords and woe be to those who don't pay the heavy toll to pass through in one piece.

The reality is that that scene depicts a breakdown so advanced that society has passed the point of no return. The truth is however that society has broken down and is no longer functioning properly. A broken social system is what you see when you look outside, sure things look normal outwardly but ask some random strangers how they are faring in this economy and darkness emerges.

A town in California recently informed its' tax payers that police will no longer be dispatched for home burglaries. In many towns across the US police and fire services have been cut back leaving the populace at risk. How long before police will no longer be dispatched for home invasion robberies where criminals hold families at gun point until they produce cash from a safe or other valuables?

Our leaders can sooth us with reports that the economy is getting better but words are cheap and unemployment is still increasing as are business failures, home foreclosures, homelessness and a litany of other social ills. Sure, the stock market is rising but who do you know that is benefiting? There is evidence that the Federal Reserve is manipulating the stock market through what has been termed P.O.M.O. or Permanent Open Market Operations. They often deny this but not convincingly. I would argue that any economic system that has to resort to such tactics is in the throes of collapse.

I see no outrage though, no pitchforks or firebrands heading up the hill in the darkness, toward the centers of power. I won't pretend to know the reasons behind this but I will say it may bode more ominous for us as it indicates that the masses won't panic until they are out of options and effectively cornered. In a system that is fundamentally broken this won't get better until the underlying problems are repaired, and I see no efforts there, which brings me to my point; the first law of panic is to panic first!

OK, maybe panic is too strong a suggestion but you get my point... Waiting until you see the determination in a desperate person's eyes is not the time to prepare for your personal security, the time to do it is now when the social weather looks relatively calm and no one is coming for you with a knife or overwhelming physical force.

I recommend a personal security kit for both the home and when you are out and about. Pepper Spray is my first choice for home defense. I choose a 9oz can of Wild Fire 18 % Oleo Resin Capsicum (Pepper) for first defense in the home or business and the1.5oz spray for personal defense when out of the house. In the home place it within easy reach from the kitchen or living-room where you can get to it fast if strangers force their way in through a door without warning. Second, for home defense I also like the 21 inch extending steel baton with optional flashlight attachment. The baton can be held in an overhand fashion to light an area and can be deployed effectively from this position for strikes and takedowns. I like the baton as with advanced instruction a person can deploy it in seemingly endless ways for a number of arm, hand and leg locks as well as take-downs without inflicting major physical damage to an assailant if you so choose.

A good home security system is also recommended but a small personal alarm is a great idea as well. These alarms come in a variety of shapes and styles, are easily carried and inexpensive. When activated they emit an ear piercing screech and can cause enough ruckus to halt an attack.

A more powerful option is a stun gun. These now come in power ranges of over 4 million volts, in sizes ranging from large flashlight/stun guns to something as small as a tube of lip-stick. My favorite is the RUNT 4.5 which is the size and shape of a pack of cigarettes, is easily carried and can be held unobtrusively in one hand. It packs a 4.5 million volt punch which, when deployed correctly, can completely incapacitate a large man.

Stun guns aren't every ones bag of chips though. For those who find them inconvenient or intimidating and pepper spray not practical to carry, I recommend the kutotan. A standard kubotan is 5 1/2 inches long, made of wood, steel or aluminum and fits nicely in the palm of the hand. You may have seen one but not known what you were looking at. The one I carry looks like an oversized cribbage pin with a key ring attached. Held tightly in one hand it can be used to swing keys at an attacker's eyes and face, or to deliver painful strikes with the butt end to any area of the body - trust me, these things hurt! It can also be used to reinforce the fist for punching. At the very least I recommend carrying a kubotan as a key-ring as an emergency escape tool if attacked. It's not fool-proof but it is better than nothing and provides a valuable option!

In the current economic climate, personal safety is a real concern and sometimes avoiding robbery or attack is simply a matter of exuding the confidence that comes with the knowledge that you are prepared; after all if you can defend yourself you don't look like a victim. If indeed you are attacked, it is important to have tools to escape. In the real world it is better to have it and not need it than to need it and not have it.

INTERVIEW #11:

Self-Defense - Get Real!

Read the headlines, watch the news, the escalation of violence and theft is apparent. It seem as the economy struggles, people get to be more and more desperate. Some of the most unlikely people are turning to crime as a way to make ends meet. Recently there were several bank robberies and convenience store hold-ups in Albuquerque, NM being perpetrated by elderly criminals. What are the odds of that? As a result of this escalation, the self-defense industry has seen growth.

More and more ordinary citizens are seeking training in different areas of self-defense and martial arts. The firearms industry has also seen a rise in the purchases of new guns and likewise the concealed carry and other training opportunities are growing. Consumers need to be aware of some of the options and avoid some of the pitfalls out there. The most important factor should be the realistic nature of the training. Is the instructor going to teach you anything or simply show you what they know.

There are significant differences in the choices that are available and the investment required in most modern self-defense programs. If the consumer is interested in self-defense (home defense, personal defense) and does not intend to commit to months and possibly years to the art, then most martial arts should not be considered. Typically, martial arts classes are taught an hour or two once or twice a week on an on going basis.

They are great as a part of a fitness regiment and for flexibility and if practiced consistently, can be useful in a self-defense situation. In most cases however, many years are required to advance in skill and level. There are programs available to the public that are based on a military model with the emphasis on teaching to the unskilled person in an accelerated format. These programs are most often considered Close Quarters Combatives. An example of one of these types of programs is SPEAR or Personal Defense Readiness.

The situation with firearm training is similar in that there are many schools and training opportunities to choose from. If the consumer does a simple search on the internet, there are classes to take offering everything from basic NRA introductory courses to post apocalyptic survival and sniper training out to one mile or more. I think that those classes would be interesting, don't get me wrong. Most of us find it necessary to be choosy about where we spend our training dollars. If you want to carry a small handgun concealed for defense of yourself and your family and have no intention of taking it any further, there are classes for that. Choose the courses that relate to your specific situation, practice diligently and master those skills, then move on if you so choose.

If you are seeking self-defense instruction, you need to do some homework and decide what you are really looking for. Do you want hand to hand fighting, a shotgun behind the door, a small pistol and a concealed carry license, or maybe a combination of all of the above. Once you make that decision, do some more research and find the appropriate instructor/facility. It is very likely that as you continue the process of educating yourself that you will want to attend other seminars and programs. This is a good thing. Self-defense is a very personal thing. lets face it, we are learning how to defend our own life. What could possibly be more personal than that?

There is someone trying to break into your home or business. You are inside and hear the commotion and decide to investigate (not a wise decision.)   Upon your approach to where you believe the noise has originated you notice a rather large person standing in the doorway and it is obvious that he has a gun…a rather large one.

Now what?   What happens to you and your emotions at that moment? Have you studied this aspect of self defense?   Are you ready for what is going to, without question, happen in the next few seconds?

No, you probably have not and that is why the next section of this book is so very important. Read on now and learn.

Tachypsychia

Tachypsychia is a neurological condition that alters the perception of time, usually induced by physical exertion, drug use, or a traumatic event. It is sometimes referred to by martial arts instructors and self-defense experts as the Tachy Psyche effect.

For someone affected by tachypsychia, time perceived by the individual either lengthens, making events appear to slow down, or contracts, objects appearing as moving in a speeding blur.

It is believed that tachypsychia is induced by a combination of high levels of dopamine and norepinephrine, usually during periods of great physical stress and/or in violent confrontation.

Physical responses

Also called the "fight or flight" response of the body to an event our mind considers life-threatening, tachypsychia is believed to include numerous physical changes.

Adrenaline response

Upon being stimulated by fear or anger, the adrenal medulla may automatically produce the hormone epinephrine (aka adrenaline) directly into the blood stream. This can have various effects on various bodily systems, including:

Increased heart rate and blood pressure. It is common for a tachypsychia subject's pulse to rise to between 200 and 300 beats per minute (bpm) Increased heart rate (above 250 bpm) can cause fainting, and the body may adduct all limbs, adopting fetal position, in preparation for a coma.

Dilation of the bronchial passages, permitting higher absorption of oxygen.

Dilated pupils to allow more light to enter, and visual exclusion—tunnel vision—occurs, allowing greater focus but resulting in the loss of peripheral vision.

Release of glucose into the bloodstream, generating extra energy by raising the blood sugar level.

It is common for an individual to experience auditory exclusion or sensitivity. It is also common for individuals to experience an increased pain tolerance, loss of color vision, short term memory loss, decreased fine motor skills, decreased communication skills, or decreased coordination.

Psychological response

The most common experience during tachypsychia is the feeling that time has either increased or slowed down, brought on by the increased brain activity cause by epinephrine, or the severe decrease in brain activity caused by the "catecholamine washout" occurring after the event.

It is common for an individual experiencing tachypsychia to have serious misinterpretations of their surroundings during the events, through a combination of their altered perception of time, as well as transient partial color blindness and tunnel vision.

After the irregularly high levels of adrenaline consumed during sympathetic nervous system activation, an individual may display signs and symptoms of post-traumatic stress disorder, and it is common for the person to display extreme emotional lability and fatigue, regardless of their actual physical exertion.

It is possible to manage tachypsychia still occurring after the event, and it is common for soldiers and martial artists to use tachypsychia in order to increase their performance during stressful situations.

Now the reason I have addressed this issue is to clearly point out the following; Yes, Head Shots Work In Any Caliber but…

Stressful situations will almost certainly NOT allow you to make the critical shot. It is matter of fact. Why is it that law enforcement officers must fire their weapons more than one time if they are well trained and able to kill a paper target 99.9% of the time? The answer is simple. Paper targets don't shoot back and don't present any type of threat. You point your weapon, squeeze the trigger and the paper person dies with two well placed shots to center mass (heart) and one nicely placed bullet to the head.

You likely noted earlier in this book that many people have been shot repeatedly in "center mass" but continued to move forward and exhibit aggressive actions that threaten the safety of someone. Yes the heart has been destroyed and in fact the person is already dead. The trouble is that the brain doesn't know it yet so continues to do what it was programmed to do, live.

Shooting someone is not to be done with the intent of killing them. No, shooting someone is done specifically to stop the aggressive action and deescalate a serious situation. Yes it is self defense but the Court will determine if you were justified in your actions. Eventually, if you've been well trained and know what you're doing whether in your home or on the street you will be vindicated. Until then though you will lose your weapon (evidence) and perhaps even spend a night in jail until your attorney gets your bail set. Either way it is not a good situation to be in. Best to be situationally aware and astute so as to avoid as best you can any kind of scenario that could result in you having to defend yourself with deadly force.

Yes, head shots work in caliber but do you really want things to get that far? I hope and pray that you do not. But if you do have to take the shot you now are far better informed than you were before you began reading this important book.

I wish you well. Be safe, be armed and most of all be ready to survive should the need arise.

If you have enjoyed reading this book perhaps you'd be interested in other books written by Thomas Woodsman. He has several available on amazon.com in Kindle E-book form.

Search for Mr. Woodsman's other books by doing a simple author search on amazon.com You will find there other books that will keep you entertained for hours upon end.